BLACK
ACHIEVEMENTS
IN ARTS AND LITERATURE

CELEBRATING GORDON PARKS,
AMANDA GORMAN, AND MORE

ELLIOTT SMITH
CICELY LEWIS, EXECUTIVE EDITOR

Lerner Publications ◆ Minneapolis

LETTER FROM CICELY LEWIS

Dear Reader,

As a girl, I wanted to be like Oprah Winfrey. She is a Black woman from Mississippi like me who became an award-winning actor, author, and businessperson. Oftentimes, history books leave out the accomplishments and contributions of people of color. When you

CICELY LEWIS

see someone who looks like you and has a similar background excelling at something, it helps you to see yourself be great.

I created Read Woke to amplify the voices of people who are often underrepresented. These books bring to light the beauty, talent, and integrity of Black people in music, activism, sports, the arts, and other areas. As you read, think about why it's important to celebrate Black excellence and the achievements of all people regardless of race, gender, or status. How did the people mentioned succeed despite barriers placed on them? How can we use these stories to inspire others?

Black excellence is everywhere in your daily life. I hope these people inspire you to never give up and continue to let your light shine.

With gratitude,

Cicely Lewis

TABLE OF CONTENTS

Poet and activist Amanda Gorman recites one of her poems during President Joe Biden's inauguration ceremony.

WORDS OF WISDOM

On January 20, 2021, twenty-two-year-old poet Amanda Gorman stepped onto the stage at President Joe Biden's inauguration ceremony. She read from her original work "The Hill We Climb": "If we merge mercy with might, and might with right, / then love becomes our legacy and change our / children's birthright."

Gorman is the country's first National Youth Poet Laureate: an honor given to writers of extraordinary talent. Gorman's work, which explores racial justice, has been praised worldwide. And on that special day, she showed how the power of words can encourage everyone to remain brave and keep working toward a better future.

This book will explore Black excellence throughout the arts and literature in the US. While not every important writer or artist is in this book, the ones highlighted here are among those who have helped shape or innovate their art form. They've also inspired the next generation of artists and writers.

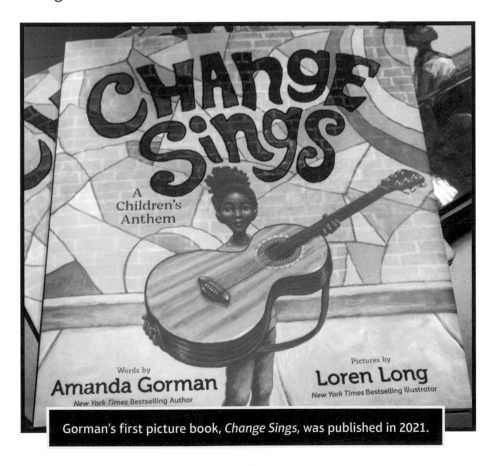

Gorman's first picture book, *Change Sings*, was published in 2021.

CHAPTER 1

BOOKS FOR CHANGE

Black writers have detailed the highs and lows of Black life. These authors broke new ground, told powerful stories, and challenged readers using their words and characters.

> "My job is to say, 'I understand. I see you.'"
>
> —JASON REYNOLDS IN 2019

SHARING HIS VOICE

When Jason Reynolds was young, music helped him find his path to writing. Encouraged by the work of his favorite rappers, Reynolds put his thoughts on paper. Even when others criticized his work, Reynolds kept writing. He is one of the most gifted writers of his time. His books have sold millions of copies and give a voice to Black youth, who are often forgotten in children's literature.

Jason Reynolds in 2017

Reynolds's magic is captured in the Track series. These four books tell a story of an elite track team. Reynolds continues to write books and poems. He has served as the National Ambassador for Young People's Literature, with the goal of connecting with kids through books and reading.

A BELOVED WRITER

Toni Morrison experienced racism as a child. But she also learned about Black heritage and folklore from her parents. She used these experiences to forge a writing career. Morrison was a teacher and editor before publishing her first book, *The Bluest Eye*, in 1970 when she was thirty-nine.

Morrison's breakthrough came with the 1987 book *Beloved*. Based on a true event that occurred during enslavement, the book won the Pulitzer Prize, an award for achievement in the arts. Morrison continued writing books that explored racial and women's issues. She won the Nobel Prize in Literature in 1993, becoming the first Black woman to earn this award given to works that benefit humankind. She continued writing until her death in 2019.

Morrison with her 1977 book, *Song of Solomon*, at an event in 2012

REFLECT

Writers often write about personal experiences. What would you write about your life?

ANGER INTO ACTION

Angie Thomas saw violence in her everyday life while growing up in Mississippi. But it was the 2009 California shooting of an unarmed Black man, Oscar Grant, that drove her to follow her writing dreams. Thomas channeled her anger into turning a short story she had already written into the 2017 book *The Hate U Give*.

In 2023 she wrote the middle grade book *Nic Blake and the Remarkables: The Manifestor Prophecy*. The fantasy book follows a young girl with magical abilities. Thomas explains she sees writing as a form of activism, giving people a chance to understand issues or cultures they may not yet know.

Angie Thomas presents her book *The Hate U Give* during an event in 2019.

DID YOU KNOW?

Roots was one of the most important books of the twentieth century. In the book, author Alex Haley (*below*) explores his own family's journey from Africa through enslavement in the US to freedom. *Roots* spent twenty-two weeks at No. 1 on the *New York Times* bestseller list.

Dancer and choreographer Alvin Ailey (*center*) performs with two other dancers in New York City in 1975.

CHAPTER 2
STRIDES IN DANCING

D ance has always been a key element of the Black experience. These dancers pushed through racism to achieve greatness, breaking boundaries to allow people to see dance in a new way:

FATHER OF DANCE

There would be no modern Black dance without Alvin Ailey. After a rough childhood, Ailey began studying dance in 1949 in Los Angeles. In 1958 he founded the Alvin Ailey American Dance Theater, which still performs to audiences worldwide. His goal was to reflect Black culture through dance.

Ailey's choreography led to great works like *Revelations* and *The River*. But one of Ailey's greatest achievements is opening doors for other dancers of color. The Ailey School started in 1969 and continues to train a new generation of dancers.

Ailey teaching a dance class

Savion Glover used elements of tap when creating his own style that he called freestyle hardcore. Glover's choreography and tap dancing have helped keep the art form alive in modern dance.

Savion Glover performing in 2004

Glover started on Broadway at ten years old in *The Tap Dance Kid*. He would go on to star in and choreograph the 1996 Broadway musical *Bring in 'da Noise, Bring in 'da Funk*, which looks at events in Black history. Glover won the Tony Award for Best Choreography, an annual award given to the best live Broadway performance. Glover tours the country, teaching tap dance to the next generation of performers.

REFLECT

What steps do you think dance studios could take to make sure everyone, regardless of race or gender, gets a chance to perform?

PRIMA BALLET DANCER

Misty Copeland shattered stereotypes about what ballet dancers should look like to succeed at the highest ranks of dance. Most principal dancers start training in ballet before the age of five. But Copeland didn't attend her first ballet class until she was thirteen. In 2015 she became the first Black principal dancer in the history of the American Ballet Theatre.

Copeland's grace and power allowed her to shine in many roles. She danced in *The Nutcracker*, *Sleeping Beauty*, and *Romeo and Juliet*. In each performance, she won positive reviews from tough critics. Copeland has used several platforms to inspire young dancers. She's written several children's books and worked with the Boys & Girls Clubs of America. This organization provides after-school programs, many in the arts, for children.

> "I'm excited to take a step back and to watch this next generation of Black and Brown dancers grow into being leaders."
>
> —MISTY COPELAND IN 2021

Misty Copeland (*right*) in the American Ballet Theatre's 2017
production of *The Nutcracker*

In 1984 photographer Gordon Parks stands next to his famous photo *American Gothic*.

CHAPTER 3
WORKS OF ART

Art is a powerful way for creative people to explore culture, history, and pride. Black artists have told their story through visual art for hundreds of years.

ETCHED IN STONE

Augusta Savage was one of the first artists in the US to focus on Black facial features. Her sculptures, often of famous Black individuals of the 1920s, were realistic. Savage's work won her several opportunities to study in Paris. In 1934 she became the first Black member of the National Association of Women Painters and Sculptors.

Her largest work, a 16-foot (5 m) sculpture called *The Harp*, was made for the 1939 New York World Fair. There was no money to make the sculpture permanent, so it was destroyed after the event. Savage lived the rest of her life largely unknown, only to gain fame for her talent years after she died in 1962.

Augusta Savage (*right*) holding a miniature version of her sculpture *The Harp*

DID YOU KNOW?

Jean-Michel Basquiat burst onto the American art scene in the 1980s. His graffiti and paintings appeared all over New York City and have been exhibited in museums and galleries. His work reflected the beginnings of hip-hop culture and commented on social issues, such as the gap between wealthy Americans and those living in poverty.

CAMERA-READY

From behind his camera, Gordon Parks captured nearly every important figure and event in Black history for more than sixty years. As a youth, Parks bought a camera and taught himself how to use it. He worked for several government agencies and later for magazines.

"I saw that the camera could be a weapon against poverty, against racism, against all sorts of social wrongs."

—GORDON PARKS

Parks took portraits of such iconic figures as Malcolm X and Muhammad Ali. He also shot such images as his 1942 *American Gothic* to highlight civil rights and poverty issues. Parks was also an author, playwright, movie director, and more. He kept working until he died in 2006. His photography remains an amazing look at Black life throughout the decades.

Parks in Paris, France, in 1985

MIXING PAST AND PRESENT

Kehinde Wiley's paintings and sculptures often place modern-looking Black and Brown men into historical portraits, creating a clash of styles in vibrant colors. Wiley takes photographs of people he finds on the street for inspiration.

Kehinde Wiley's sculpture *Rumors of War* is displayed in New York City in 2019.

REFLECT

There are many forms of art, and what cultures regard as art changes over time. What do you consider to be art?

In 2017 Barack Obama chose Wiley to paint his presidential portrait. The result shows a relaxed president surrounded by colorful flowers that represent points in his life. Wiley also created a piece in response to the removal of Confederate monuments across the US. During the US Civil War, the Confederacy was made up of the states that wanted to keep slavery in the United States. Wiley's sculpture *Rumors of War* is of a modern Black man riding a horse. It's displayed in Richmond, Virginia, the former capital of the Confederacy.

Kehinde Wiley (*left*) with Barack Obama in 2018 during the unveiling at the National Portrait Gallery in Washington, DC, of the presidential portrait Wiley painted of Obama

Poet Nikki Giovanni performs at the 2016 Afropunk Brooklyn Festival.

CHAPTER 4
SPEAKING CLEARLY

As Amanda Gorman showed, the power of the spoken word can be used to great effect. Many legendary Black artists conveyed empowerment and freedom using poetry and plays.

PURE POET

As a child, Nikki Giovanni wanted to do something no one else had. She decided to become a poet. Giovanni emerged in the 1960s as part of the Black Arts Movement, a period focused on showing cultural pride. Giovanni's poems focus on Black history and equality. But they are often about her childhood.

In one of her most famous poems, "Nikki-Rosa," she writes: "Black love is Black wealth and they'll / probably talk about my hard childhood / and never understand that / all the while I was quite happy."

Giovanni wrote many collections of poetry.

REFLECT

Which writers do you like? How have their books or poems impacted you?

A BRIGHT LIGHT

From an early age, Lorraine Hansberry broke barriers. She attended the University of Wisconsin–Madison, where she integrated a dormitory. She then moved to New York to become a writer. There she created her master work, *A Raisin in the Sun*, which premiered on Broadway in 1959.

Hansberry became the first Black woman to have a play produced for Broadway. The play, which centers on a Black family fighting against racism and housing discrimination, is widely considered to be one of the best plays ever. Hansberry also wrote the screenplay for its 1961 movie adaptation.

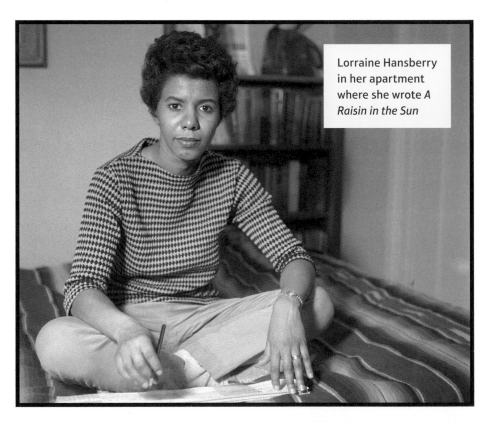

Lorraine Hansberry in her apartment where she wrote *A Raisin in the Sun*

DID YOU KNOW?

Maya Angelou (*below*) is one of the world's most well-known writers. Her book *I Know Why the Caged Bird Sings* is her most famous work, and she is also known for her volumes of poetry. Her poem "Still I Rise" powerfully encourages the triumph of the spirit. Angelou died in 2014 at the age of eighty-six, leaving behind work that has made a great impact on the world.

CYCLE OF LIFE

When August Wilson became a playwright, he wrote about the place he called home. Wilson's Pittsburgh Cycle, a collection of ten plays, explores the Black experience in the 1900s. Written over twenty years and featuring recurring characters, buildings, and symbols, the plays were Wilson's life work.

His play *Fences* won the Tony Award and a Pulitzer Prize. *The Piano Lesson* earned a second Pulitzer. Wilson's works shined a light on the everyday life of its Black characters.

August Wilson has twice won the Pulitzer Prize.

FUTURE ARTISTS

Whether it's writing, dance, painting, or other art, Black artists continue to shine in arts and literature. Explore the works of past and present artists. Think about the kinds of art that move and change you.

Dancers from the Alvin Ailey American Dance Theater perform in 2021.

GLOSSARY

adaptation: a movie or play that has been adapted from a written work

choreography: a set of steps and movements in dance

discrimination: unfair treatment of a particular group of people

folklore: beliefs, customs, and stories of a community

heritage: beliefs and ideas that come from a person's family or ethnic background

inauguration: the beginning of a presidency

innovate: to make change by introducing new methods or ideas

integrate: the practice of bringing together people of different races as equals in a space or organization

laureate: a person honored for achievement in an area

poverty: the condition of not having enough money or resources to meet basic needs

stereotype: a widely held—but unrealistically simple—image or idea of a specific thing

SOURCE NOTES

4   Jennifer Liu, "Read the Full Text of Amanda Gorman's Inaugural Poem 'The Hill We Climb,'" CNBC Make It, January 20, 2021, https://www.cnbc.com/2021/01/20/amanda-gormans-inaugural-poem-the-hill-we-climb-full-text.html.

7   Concepción de León, "Jason Reynolds Is on a Mission," *New York Times*, last modified October 29, 2019, https://www.nytimes.com/2019/10/28/books/jason-reynolds-look-both-ways.html.

14   Erin Vanderhoof, "Misty Copeland on How Seeing Herself as a Black Ballerina Made Her a Better Artist," *Vanity Fair*, October 28, 2021, https://www.vanityfair.com/style/2021/10/misty-copeland-black-ballerinas-interview.

18   "Biography," Gordon Parks Foundation, accessed August 8, 2022, https://www.gordonparksfoundation.org/gordon-parks/biography.

23   Nikki Giovanni, "Nikki-Rosa," Poetry Foundation, accessed August 18, 2022, https://www.poetryfoundation.org/poems/48219/nikki-rosa.

READ WOKE READING LIST

Britannica Kids: Amanda Gorman
https://kids.britannica.com/kids/article/Amanda-Gorman/633195

Copeland, Misty. *Life in Motion: An Unlikely Ballerina*. New York: Aladdin Books, 2022.

Duling, Kaitlyn. *Alvin Ailey*. Vero Beach, FL: Rourke Educational Media, 2022.

Kehinde Wiley Studio
https://kehindewiley.com

Poetry Foundation: Maya Angelou
https://www.poetryfoundation.org/poets/maya-angelou

Smith, Elliott. *Black Achievements in Entertainment: Celebrating Hattie McDaniel, Chadwick Boseman, and More*. Minneapolis: Lerner Publications, 2024.

Tyner, Dr. Artika R. *Amanda Gorman: Inspiring Hope with Poetry*. Minneapolis: Lerner Publications, 2022.

INDEX

PHOTO ACKNOWLEDGMENTS

Image credits: Rob Carr/Getty Images News/Getty Images, p. 4; Patti McConville/Alamy Stock Photo, p. 5; Roger Tillberg/Alamy Stock Photo, p. 6; Desiree Navarro/WireImage/Getty Images, p. 7; Patrick Kovarik/AFP/Getty Images, p. 8; Marla Aufmuth/Getty Images Entertainment/Getty Images, p. 9; Bettmann/Getty Images, pp. 10, 17; Afro American Newspapers/Gado/Getty Images, p. 11; Vic de Lucia/Archive Photos/Getty Images, p. 12; Peter Kramer/Getty Images Entertainmen/Getty Images, p. 13; MediaNews Group/Orange County Register/Getty Images, p. 15; John Pineda/Hulton Archive/Getty Images, p. 16; Frederic Reglain/Gamma-Rapho/Getty Images, p. 19; Spencer Platt/Getty Images News/Getty Images, p. 20; Saul Loeb/AFP/Getty Images, p. 21; Kris Connor/Getty Images Entertainment/Getty Images, p. 22; Michael Ochs Archives/Stringer/Getty Images, p. 23; David Attie/Michael Ochs Archives/Getty Images, p. 24; Bennett Raglin/WireImage/Getty Images, p. 25; Boston Globe/Getty Images, p. 26; Timothy A. Clary/AFP/Getty Images, p. 27. Design elements: Anastasiia Gevko/Shutterstock. Cicely Lewis portrait photos by Fernando Decillis.

Cover: Serena Xu-Ning/Alamy Stock Photo (Amanda Gorman); Globe Photos/ZUMAPRESS.com/Alamy Stock Photo (Gordon Parks).

Lerner Publications Company
An imprint of Lerner Publishing Group, Inc.
241 First Avenue North
Minneapolis, MN 55401 USA

For reading levels and more information, look up this title at www.lernerbooks.com.

Main body text set in Aptifer Sans LT Pro.
Typeface provided by Linotype AG.

Editor: Brianna Kaiser **Designer:** Kim Morales **Photo Editor:** Annie Zheng

Library of Congress Cataloging-in-Publication Data

Names: Smith, Elliott, 1976– author.
Title: Black achievements in arts and literature : celebrating Gordon Parks, Amanda Gorman, and more / Elliott Smith.
Description: Minneapolis, MN : Lerner Publications Company, [2023] | Series: Black excellence project (read woke books) | Includes bibliographical references and index. | Audience: Ages 9–14 | Audience: Grades 4–6 | Summary: "There are many forms of art and literature. Learn about Black people who have excelled in literature and the arts, including author Jason Reynolds, dancer Misty Copeland, and painter Kehinde Wiley"—Provided by publisher.
Identifiers: LCCN 2022038361 (print) | LCCN 2022038362 (ebook) | ISBN 9781728486642 (library binding) | ISBN 9781728499963 (paperback) | ISBN 9781728496146 (ebook)
Subjects: LCSH: African American artists—Juvenile literature.
Classification: LCC NX512.3.A35 S65 2023 (print) | LCC NX512.3.A35 (ebook) | DDC 709.2/396073—dc23/eng20230119

LC record available at https://lccn.loc.gov/2022038361
LC ebook record available at https://lccn.loc.gov/2022038362

Manufactured in the United States of America
1-52594-50768-1/11/2023